This book belongs to:

MY Stitchy LIST

1. _____
2. _____
3. _____
4. _____
5. _____
6. _____
7. _____
8. _____
9. _____
10. _____
11. _____
12. _____
13. _____
14. _____
15. _____
16. _____
17. _____
18. _____
19. _____
20. _____
21. _____
22. _____
23. _____
24. _____
25. _____

MY Stitchy LIST

26. _____
27. _____
28. _____
29. _____
30. _____
31. _____
32. _____
33. _____
34. _____
35. _____
36. _____
37. _____
38. _____
39. _____
40. _____
41. _____
42. _____
43. _____
44. _____
45. _____
46. _____
47. _____
48. _____
49. _____
50. _____

PROJECT #1

Pattern Name: _____

Pattern Designer: _____

Start Date: _____ End Date: _____

Stitched On: _____

Stitch Count: _____

Stitched Size: _____

Floss:

Time Tracker:

Notes:

xxxxxxxxxxxxxxxxxxxxxxxxxxx

PROJECT #2

Pattern Name: _____
Pattern Designer: _____

Start Date: _____ End Date: _____

Stitched On: _____
Stitch Count: _____
Stitched Size: _____

Floss:

Time Tracker:

Notes:

PROJECT #3

Pattern Name: _____
Pattern Designer: _____

Start Date: _____ End Date: _____

Stitched On: _____
Stitch Count: _____
Stitched Size: _____

Floss:

Time Tracker:

Notes:

PROJECT #4

Pattern Name: _____
Pattern Designer: _____

Start Date: _____ End Date: _____

Stitched On: _____
Stitch Count: _____
Stitched Size: _____

Floss:

Time Tracker:

Notes:

PROJECT #5

Pattern Name: _____

Pattern Designer: _____

Start Date: _____ End Date: _____

Stitched On: _____

Stitch Count: _____

Stitched Size: _____

Floss:

Time Tracker:

Notes:

PROJECT #6

Pattern Name: _____
Pattern Designer: _____

Start Date: _____ End Date: _____

Stitched On: _____
Stitch Count: _____
Stitched Size: _____

Floss:

Time Tracker:

Notes:

xxxxxxxxxxxxxxxxxxxxx

PROJECT #7

Pattern Name: _____
Pattern Designer: _____

Start Date: _____ End Date: _____

Stitched On: _____
Stitch Count: _____
Stitched Size: _____

Floss:

Time Tracker:

Notes:

xxxxxxxxxxxxxxxxxx

PROJECT #8

Pattern Name: _____
Pattern Designer: _____

Start Date: _____ End Date: _____

Stitched On: _____
Stitch Count: _____
Stitched Size: _____

Floss:

Time Tracker:

Notes:

x x x x x x x x x x x x x x x x x

PROJECT #9

Pattern Name: _____
Pattern Designer: _____

Start Date: _____ End Date: _____

Stitched On: _____
Stitch Count: _____
Stitched Size: _____

Floss:

Time Tracker:

Notes:

x x x x x x x x x x x x x x x x x

… … … … … … … … … … PROJECT #10 … … … … … … … … … …

Pattern Name: _____
Pattern Designer: _____

Start Date: _____ End Date: _____

Stitched On: _____
Stitch Count: _____
Stitched Size: _____

Floss:

Time Tracker:

Notes:

x x x x x x x x x x x x x x x x x x x x

PROJECT #11

Pattern Name: _____
Pattern Designer: _____

Start Date: _____ End Date: _____

Stitched On: _____
Stitch Count: _____
Stitched Size: _____

Floss:

Time Tracker:

Notes:

PROJECT #12

Pattern Name: _____
Pattern Designer: _____

Start Date: _____ End Date: _____

Stitched On: _____
Stitch Count: _____
Stitched Size: _____

Floss:

Time Tracker:

Notes:

x x x x x x x x x x x x x x x x x x x x

PROJECT #13

Pattern Name: _____
Pattern Designer: _____

Start Date: _____ End Date: _____

Stitched On: _____
Stitch Count: _____
Stitched Size: _____

Floss:

Time Tracker:

Notes:

PROJECT #14

Pattern Name: _____
Pattern Designer: _____

Start Date: _____ End Date: _____

Stitched On: _____
Stitch Count: _____
Stitched Size: _____

Floss:

Time Tracker:

Notes:

X X X X X X X X X X X X X X X X X X

PROJECT #15

Pattern Name: _____
Pattern Designer: _____

Start Date: _____ End Date: _____

Stitched On: _____
Stitch Count: _____
Stitched Size: _____

Floss:

Time Tracker:

Notes:

X X X X X X X X X X X X X X X X X X

PROJECT #16

Pattern Name: _____
Pattern Designer: _____

Start Date: _____ End Date: _____

Stitched On: _____
Stitch Count: _____
Stitched Size: _____

Floss:

Time Tracker:

Notes:

xxxxxxxxxxxxxxxxxxxxxxx

PROJECT #17

Pattern Name: _____
Pattern Designer: _____

Start Date: _____ End Date: _____

Stitched On: _____
Stitch Count: _____
Stitched Size: _____

Floss:

Time Tracker:

Notes:

PROJECT #18

Pattern Name: _____
Pattern Designer: _____

Start Date: _____ End Date: _____

Stitched On: _____
Stitch Count: _____
Stitched Size: _____

Floss:

Time Tracker:

Notes:

x x x x x x x x x x x x x x x x x x

PROJECT #19

Pattern Name: _____
Pattern Designer: _____

Start Date: _____ End Date: _____

Stitched On: _____
Stitch Count: _____
Stitched Size: _____

Floss:

Time Tracker:

Notes:

PROJECT #20

Pattern Name: _____
Pattern Designer: _____

Start Date: _____ End Date: _____

Stitched On: _____
Stitch Count: _____
Stitched Size: _____

Floss:

Time Tracker:

Notes:

PROJECT #21

Pattern Name: _____
Pattern Designer: _____

Start Date: _____ End Date: _____

Stitched On: _____
Stitch Count: _____
Stitched Size: _____

Floss:

Time Tracker:

Notes:

PROJECT #22

Pattern Name: _____
Pattern Designer: _____

Start Date: _____ End Date: _____

Stitched On: _____
Stitch Count: _____
Stitched Size: _____

Floss:

Time Tracker:

Notes:

PROJECT #23

Pattern Name: _____
Pattern Designer: _____

Start Date: _____ End Date: _____

Stitched On: _____
Stitch Count: _____
Stitched Size: _____

Floss:

Time Tracker:

Notes:

PROJECT #24

Pattern Name: _____
Pattern Designer: _____

Start Date: _____ End Date: _____

Stitched On: _____
Stitch Count: _____
Stitched Size: _____

Floss:

Time Tracker:

Notes:

x x x x x x x x x x x x x x x x x x x

PROJECT #25

Pattern Name: _____
Pattern Designer: _____

Start Date: _____ End Date: _____

Stitched On: _____
Stitch Count: _____
Stitched Size: _____

Floss:

Time Tracker:

Notes:

× × × × × × × × × × × × × × × × × ×

PROJECT #26

Pattern Name: _____
Pattern Designer: _____

Start Date: _____ End Date: _____

Stitched On: _____
Stitch Count: _____
Stitched Size: _____

Floss:

Time Tracker:

Notes:

XXXXXXXXXXXXXXXXXXXXX

PROJECT #27

Pattern Name: _____
Pattern Designer: _____

Start Date: _____ End Date: _____

Stitched On: _____
Stitch Count: _____
Stitched Size: _____

Floss:

Time Tracker:

Notes:

PROJECT #28

Pattern Name: _____
Pattern Designer: _____

Start Date: _____ End Date: _____

Stitched On: _____
Stitch Count: _____
Stitched Size: _____

Floss:

Time Tracker:

Notes:

x x x x x x x x x x x x x x x x x x

PROJECT #29

Pattern Name: _____
Pattern Designer: _____

Start Date: _____ End Date: _____

Stitched On: _____
Stitch Count: _____
Stitched Size: _____

Floss:

Time Tracker:

Notes:

PROJECT #30

Pattern Name: _____
Pattern Designer: _____

Start Date: _____ End Date: _____

Stitched On: _____
Stitch Count: _____
Stitched Size: _____

Floss:

Time Tracker:

Notes:

x x x x x x x x x x x x x x x x x x x x

PROJECT #31

Pattern Name: _____

Pattern Designer: _____

Start Date: _____ End Date: _____

Stitched On: _____

Stitch Count: _____

Stitched Size: _____

Floss:

Time Tracker:

Notes:

PROJECT #32

Pattern Name: _____
Pattern Designer: _____

Start Date: _____ End Date: _____

Stitched On: _____
Stitch Count: _____
Stitched Size: _____

Floss:

Time Tracker:

Notes:

x x x x x x x x x x x x x x x x x x x x

PROJECT #33

Pattern Name: _____
Pattern Designer: _____

Start Date: _____ End Date: _____

Stitched On: _____
Stitch Count: _____
Stitched Size: _____

Floss:

Time Tracker:

Notes:

X X X X X X X X X X X X X X X X X

PROJECT #34

Pattern Name: _____
Pattern Designer: _____

Start Date: _____ End Date: _____

Stitched On: _____
Stitch Count: _____
Stitched Size: _____

Floss:

Time Tracker:

Notes:

PROJECT #35

Pattern Name: _____
Pattern Designer: _____

Start Date: _____ End Date: _____

Stitched On: _____
Stitch Count: _____
Stitched Size: _____

Floss:

Time Tracker:

Notes:

PROJECT #36

Pattern Name: _____
Pattern Designer: _____

Start Date: _____ End Date: _____

Stitched On: _____
Stitch Count: _____
Stitched Size: _____

Floss:

Time Tracker:

Notes:

PROJECT #37

Pattern Name: _____
Pattern Designer: _____

Start Date: _____ End Date: _____

Stitched On: _____
Stitch Count: _____
Stitched Size: _____

Floss:

Time Tracker:

Notes:

PROJECT #38

Pattern Name: _____
Pattern Designer: _____

Start Date: _____ End Date: _____

Stitched On: _____
Stitch Count: _____
Stitched Size: _____

Floss:

Time Tracker:

Notes:

x x x x x x x x x x x x x x x x x x x x x

PROJECT #39

Pattern Name: _____
Pattern Designer: _____

Start Date: _____ End Date: _____

Stitched On: _____
Stitch Count: _____
Stitched Size: _____

Floss:

Time Tracker:

Notes:

x x x x x x x x x x x x x x x x x x

PROJECT #40

Pattern Name: _____
Pattern Designer: _____

Start Date: _____ End Date: _____

Stitched On: _____
Stitch Count: _____
Stitched Size: _____

Floss:

Time Tracker:

Notes:

x x x x x x x x x x x x x x x x x x x x

PROJECT #41

Pattern Name: _____
Pattern Designer: _____

Start Date: _____ End Date: _____

Stitched On: _____
Stitch Count: _____
Stitched Size: _____

Floss:

Time Tracker:

Notes:

PROJECT #42

Pattern Name: _____
Pattern Designer: _____

Start Date: _____ End Date: _____

Stitched On: _____
Stitch Count: _____
Stitched Size: _____

Floss:

Time Tracker:

Notes:

x x x x x x x x x x x x x x x x x x

PROJECT #43

Pattern Name: _____
Pattern Designer: _____

Start Date: _____ End Date: _____

Stitched On: _____
Stitch Count: _____
Stitched Size: _____

Floss:

Time Tracker:

Notes:

PROJECT #44

Pattern Name: _____
Pattern Designer: _____

Start Date: _____ End Date: _____

Stitched On: _____
Stitch Count: _____
Stitched Size: _____

Floss:

Time Tracker:

Notes:

x x x x x x x x x x x x x x x x x x x x

PROJECT #45

Pattern Name: _____
Pattern Designer: _____

Start Date: _____ End Date: _____

Stitched On: _____
Stitch Count: _____
Stitched Size: _____

Floss:

Time Tracker:

Notes:

PROJECT #46

Pattern Name: _____
Pattern Designer: _____

Start Date: _____ End Date: _____

Stitched On: _____
Stitch Count: _____
Stitched Size: _____

Floss:

Time Tracker:

Notes:

PROJECT #47

Pattern Name: _____
Pattern Designer: _____

Start Date: _____ End Date: _____

Stitched On: _____
Stitch Count: _____
Stitched Size: _____

Floss:

Time Tracker:

Notes:

x x x x x x x x x x x x x x x x x x x x

PROJECT #48

Pattern Name: _____
Pattern Designer: _____

Start Date: _____ End Date: _____

Stitched On: _____
Stitch Count: _____
Stitched Size: _____

Floss:

Time Tracker:

Notes:

PROJECT #49

Pattern Name: _____
Pattern Designer: _____

Start Date: _____ End Date: _____

Stitched On: _____
Stitch Count: _____
Stitched Size: _____

Floss:

Time Tracker:

Notes:

xxxxxxxxxxxxxxxxxxxxxxxxxxx

PROJECT #50

Pattern Name: _____
Pattern Designer: _____

Start Date: _____ End Date: _____

Stitched On: _____
Stitch Count: _____
Stitched Size: _____

Floss:

Time Tracker:

Notes:

MY Thread INVENTORY

MY *Thread* INVENTORY

My Notes